AF483841

Just Let $%#&! Go!

For Those Who Need That Little Extra Kick in the Pants!

By Heather and Karen Tobin

Printed in the United States of America

First Printing, 2022

ISBN 9798218080471 (Heather and Karen Tobin)

Printed by Ingram Spark

For more information, contact:
brutaltruthbooks@gmail.com

"Letting go is such an important and sometimes difficult part of life. So often we do it with our eyes closed, through gritted teeth. These authors take a lighthearted Dr. Seusian tone as they invite us to take a deep breath and just DO IT—with eyes open and maybe, with a little help from them, a little smile."

Mary Woznysmith, LCSW-C

Special Thanks

We would like to thank our parents and sister Stephanie, and our girls Anastasia and Abigail. A special thanks as well to Keri Barnum, Lynn Schwartz, Shirley Hopkins, Azante, and Kiersten Gallagher for your guidance. In addition, we thank our Uncle Ron and Joan Fox for their lifelong support.

We would like to dedicate this book to the memory of our cousins Lesley Fox Denny and Steven Fox, whose contagious laughter and brilliance lit up this world.

Foreword

"We teach best what we need to learn."
—Richard Bach

We have always loved this quote and creating this book has been an exercise in doing this very thing, teaching what we know. As many of you reading this grapple with the often brutal task of letting go, we Tobin sisters know your pain. We have lived it. The last few years have necessitated much letting go from losses of beloved family and friends to the new parameters of living during a global pandemic. We have also had to let go of self-limiting beliefs, of stuff gathering in our closets and spaces that no longer serve us. Letting Go has become our mantra whether we have liked it or not. We have written and illustrated this book to guide you gently into releasing that which no longer serves you. We sisters have found the acts of letting go are far more bearable and doable with humor and community. It is our utmost hope that in your journey of releasing the emotions, the physical stuff, the pain, or whatever you face, that this book will serve as a warm, funny friend cheering you on. Together we more easily can let go, making way for a brighter, and lighter today and tomorrow.

Karen and Heather Tobin

Are you holding on to something,
With a python's coiled grip?
Do you carry too much with you,
Although it makes you sick?

Are you dazed and distracted?
You feel your life's a wreck,
Repeat the same old story?
Loved ones want to wring your neck!

Well here's a little book for you,
Because trust me we all know,

It's time now to surrender,
And just let $%#&! go!

To let go isn't easy,
But you have what it takes…

You may fall a few steps back,
And make some more mistakes!

But you will feel a huge relief,
And seeds of peace you'll sow,

When you release your burdens,
And just let $%#&! go!

Let go of your resentments,
Even if you think you're right,

Release all of all those big worries,
That keep you up at night.

Let go of chasing all the ones,
Who do not answer back,

Let go of your obsessions,
That throw you far off track.

Let go of your self-sabotage,
It's time now to forgive.

Let go so you can be here now,
Let go so you can live!

When you hold on to things too tight,
Your hopes may not come true.

When you smother anything too much,
It runs away from you!

If you have a situation,
That snags you by the toe,

Try stopping with the pining,
And just $%#&! let it go!

When you hang on to clutter,
The toys, the clothes, the stuff,

It eventually crushes you,
Because you have too much!
So....

Polish up and sell that ring,
You've kept since the divorce,

Use the funds to take a trip,
And chart a brand new course!

Toss those things you never use,
Donate unopened gifts,

Remember, this is all just stuff,
Life's so much more than this!

Let go of all the mean self-talk,
While gazing in the mirror,

Affirm your worth, stay positive,
And you'll see so much clearer!

Let go of that old high school grudge,
Those friends who let you down,

Don't let the past imprison you,
Let go before you drown!

Let go of wanting to be "in,"
The group that left you out,

Seek out those who welcome you,
Cause that's what life's about!

Let go of all comparisons,
Of who has what next door,

Grass isn't always greener Dear,
Stop thinking you need more!

Let go of thinking you're behind,
On the winding road of life,

The joy is in the journey, friend,
Embrace both joy and strife!

And then when you're not trying,
To reel your wishes in,

Better things will come to you,
And you will let them in…

You'll attract the things you need,
At a healthier vibration,

You'll be a living radio,
Tuned to a better station!

You'll be amazed at all that is,
Just trust life's natural flow.

Begin the climb, the needed change,
And just let $%#&! go!

The End